ED EMBERLEY'S DRAWING BOOK of FACES

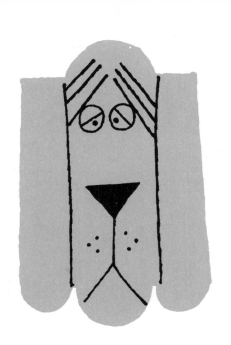
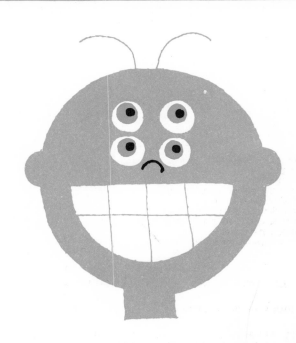
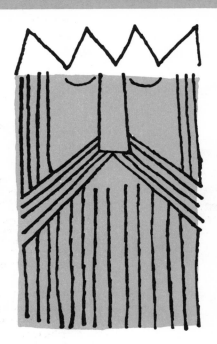

LITTLE, BROWN AND COMPANY ⊙ BOSTON AND TORONTO

► OTHER BOOKS BY ED EMBERLEY:
THE WING ON A FLEA (A BOOK ABOUT SHAPES),
GREEN SAYS GO (A BOOK ABOUT COLOR),
ED EMBERLEY'S DRAWING BOOK OF ANIMALS,
ED EMBERLEY'S DRAWING BOOK, MAKE A WORLD,
ED EMBERLEY'S LITTLE DRAWING BOOK OF:
TRAINS,
WEIRDOS,
BIRDS,
FARMS.

FOURTH PRINTING

T 04/75

LIBRARY OF CONGRESS CATALOGING IN PUBLICATION DATA

EMBERLEY, ED.
    ED EMBERLEY'S DRAWING BOOK OF FACES

    INCLUDES INDEX.
    SUMMARY: SIMPLE STEP-BY-STEP INSTRUCTIONS FOR
    DRAWING A WIDE VARIETY OF FACES REFLECTING
    VARIOUS EMOTIONS AND PROFESSIONS.

    I. FACE IN ART.   2. DRAWING -- INSTRUCTION.
[I. DRAWING -- INSTRUCTION] I. TITLE. II. TITLE:
DRAWING BOOK OF FACES
NC770.E42   743'.49   74-32033
ISBN 0-316-23609-8 LIB. BDG.

PUBLISHED SIMULTANEOUSLY IN CANADA
BY LITTLE, BROWN AND COMPANY (CANADA) LIMITED

PRINTED IN THE UNITED STATES OF AMERICA

2

IF YOU CAN DRAW THESE THINGS→ •∪◗○△◻︎wwwe
YOU CAN DRAW ALL KINDS OF FACES.
EASY STEP BY STEP DRAWINGS SHOW YOU HOW.
THIS ROW SHOWS WHAT TO DRAW.
THIS ROW SHOWS WHERE TO PUT IT.

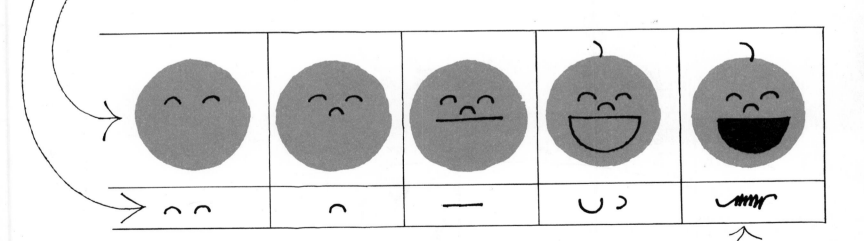

THIS SIGN MEANS "FILL IN"

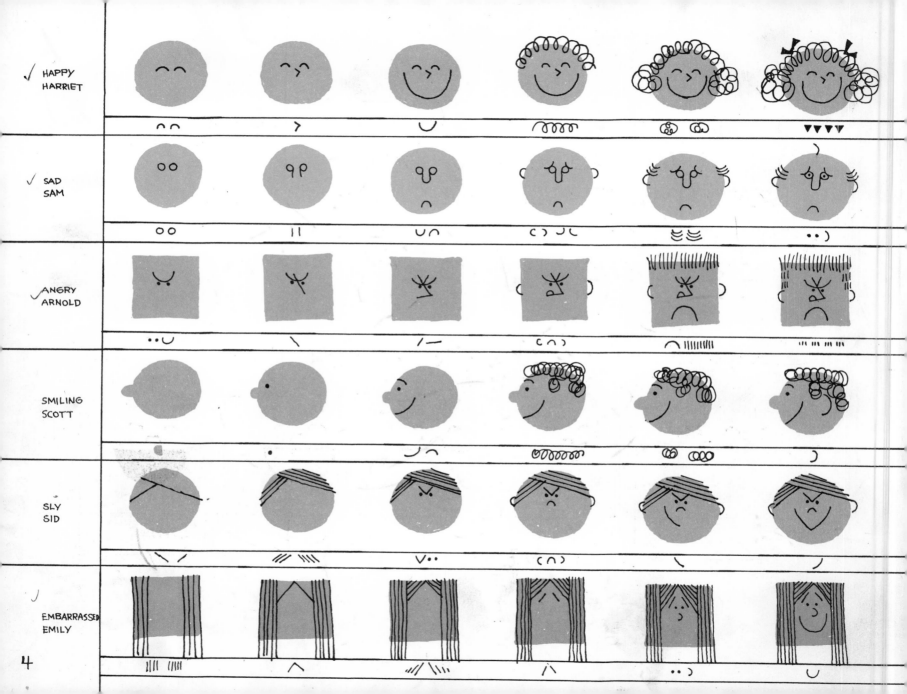

HAPPY HARRIET

SAD SAM

ANGRY ARNOLD

SMILING SCOTT

SLY SID

EMBARRASSED EMILY

4

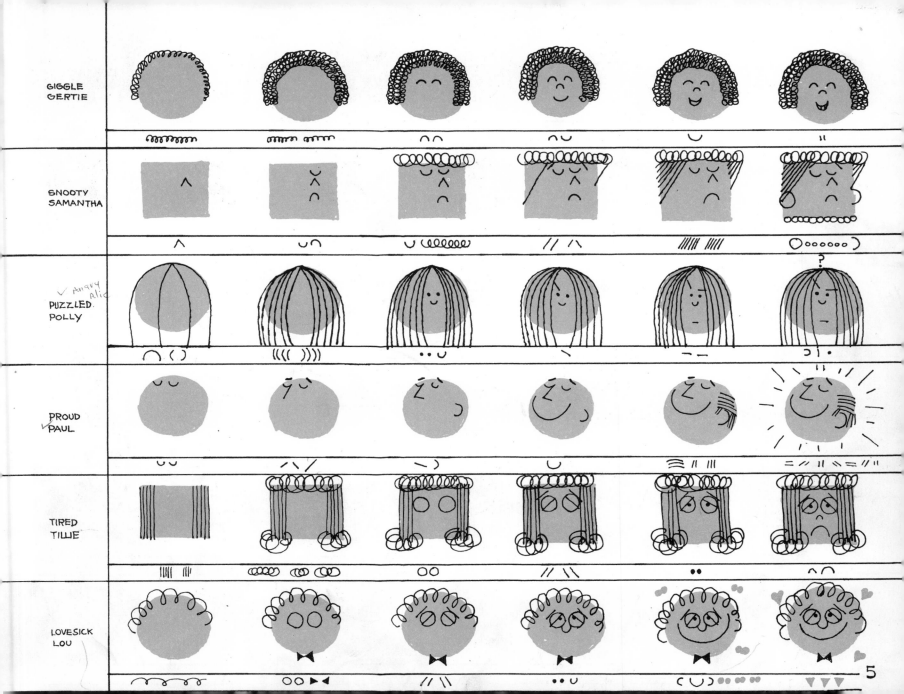

GIGGLE GERTIE

SNOOTY SAMANTHA

PUZZLED POLLY

PROUD PAUL

TIRED TILLIE

LOVESICK LOU

5

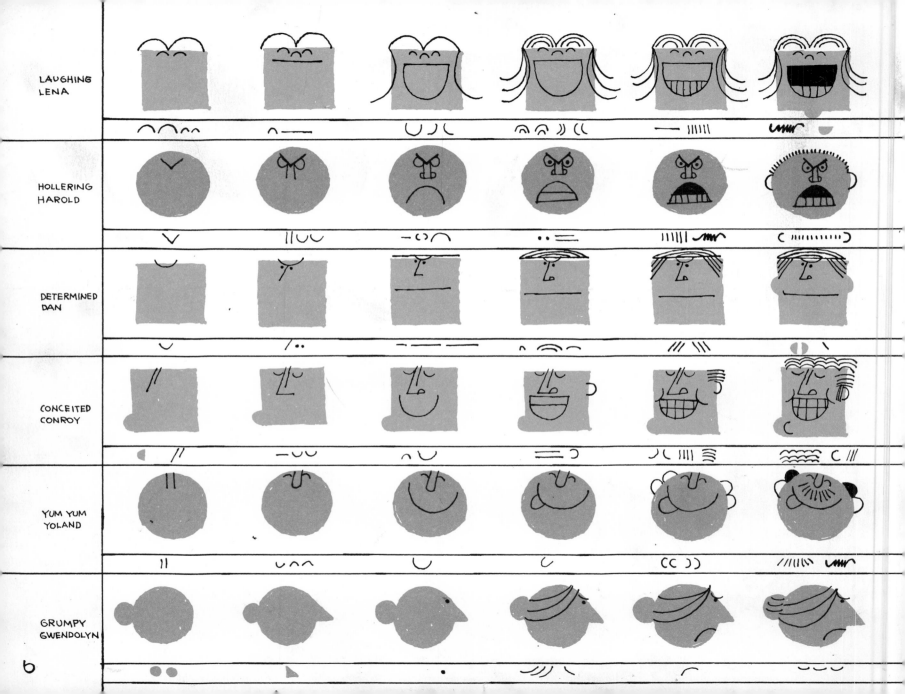

LAUGHING
LENA

HOLLERING
HAROLD

DETERMINED
DAN

CONCEITED
CONROY

YUM YUM
YOLAND

GRUMPY
GWENDOLYN

6

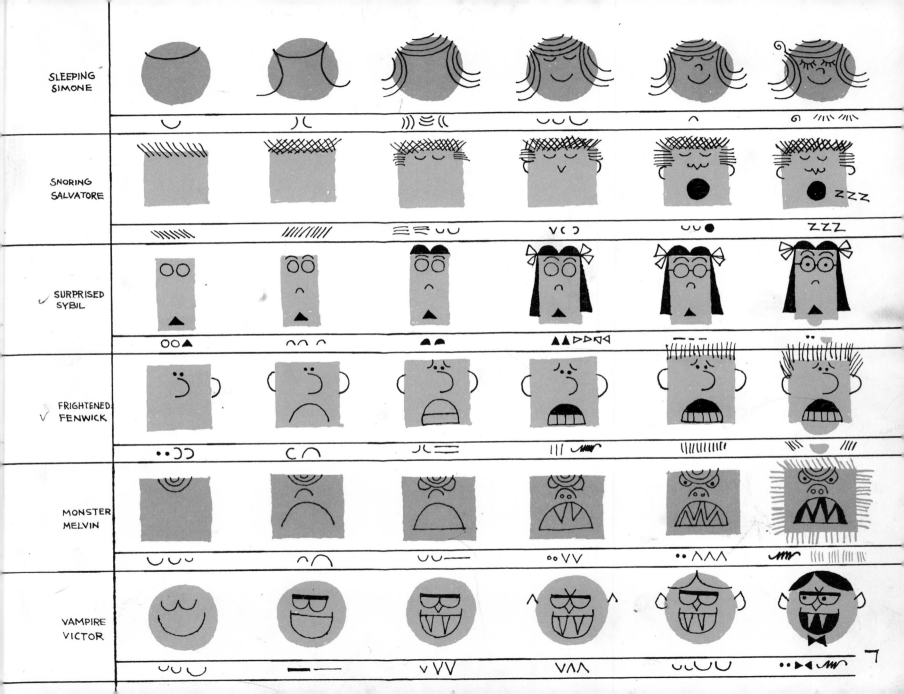

SLEEPING
SIMONE

SNORING
SALVATORE

SURPRISED
SYBIL

FRIGHTENED
FENWICK

MONSTER
MELVIN

VAMPIRE
VICTOR

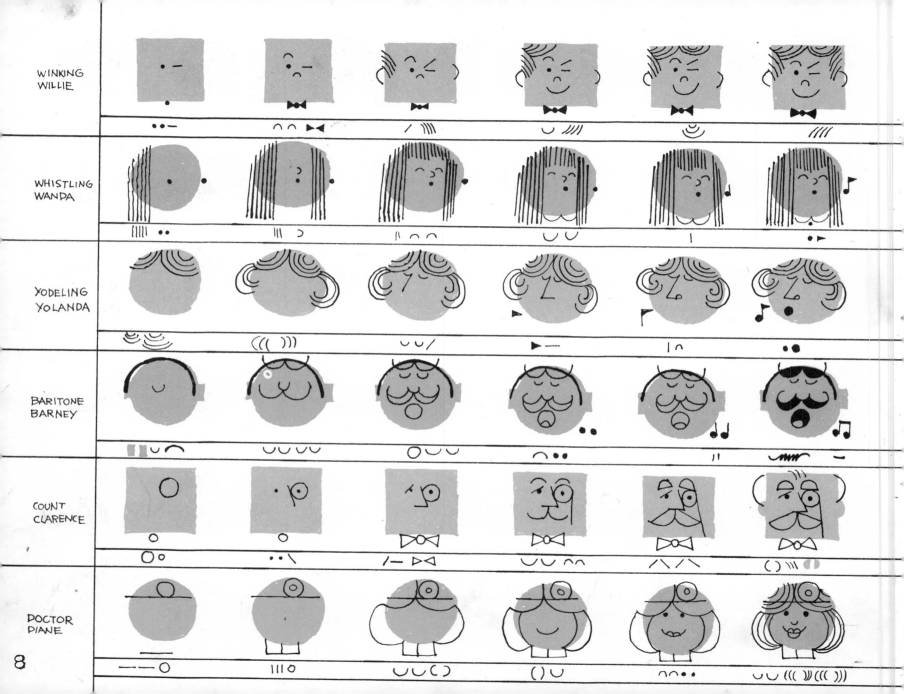

WINKING
WILLIE

WHISTLING
WANDA

YODELING
YOLANDA

BARITONE
BARNEY

COUNT
CLARENCE

DOCTOR
DIANE

8

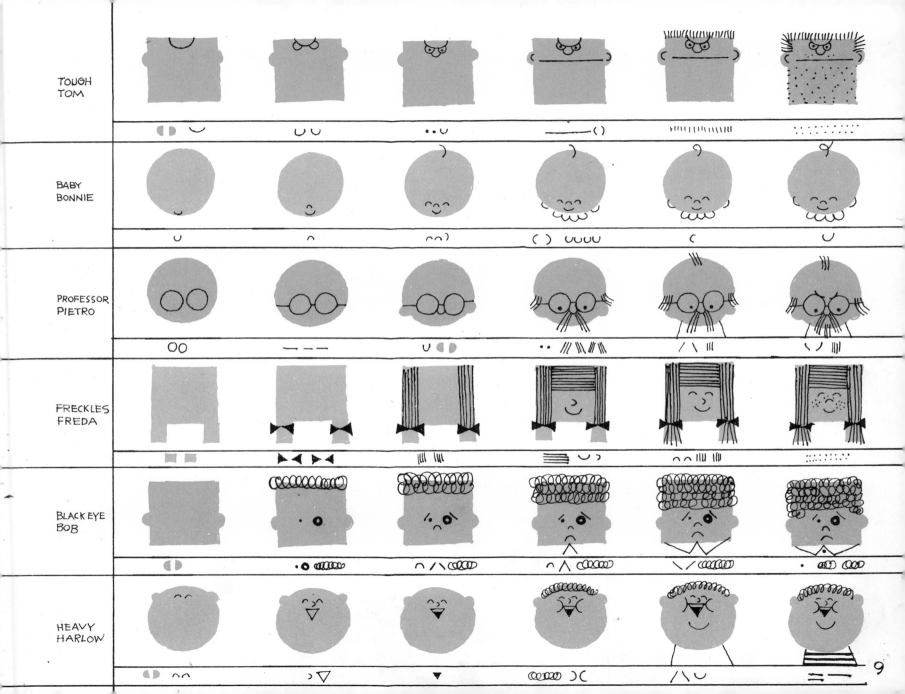

TOUGH
TOM

BABY
BONNIE

PROFESSOR
PIETRO

FRECKLES
FREDA

BLACK EYE
BOB

HEAVY
HARLOW

9

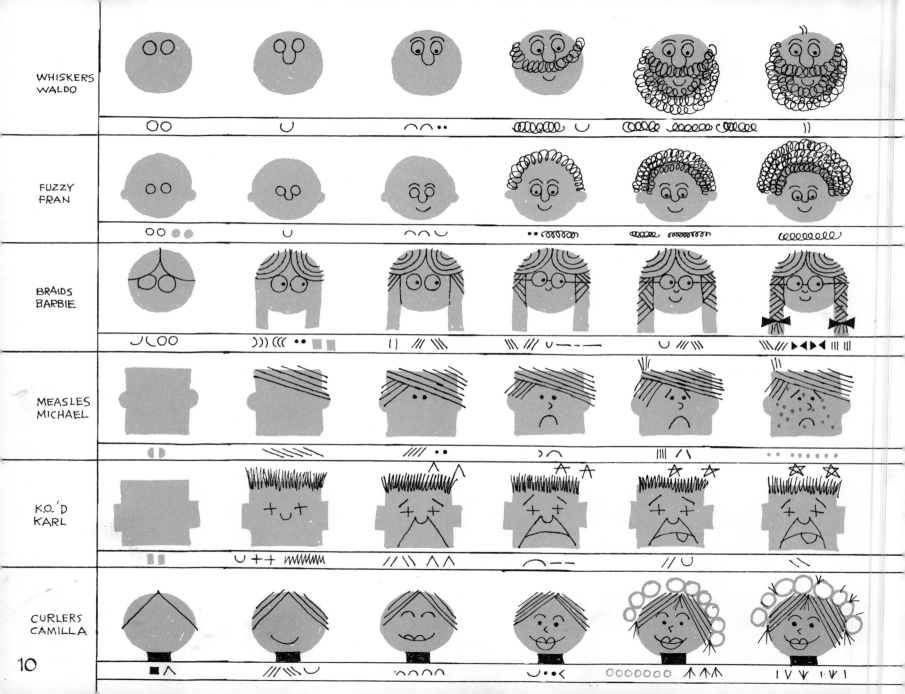

WHISKERS
WALDO

FUZZY
FRAN

BRAIDS
BARBIE

MEASLES
MICHAEL

K.O.'D
KARL

CURLERS
CAMILLA

10

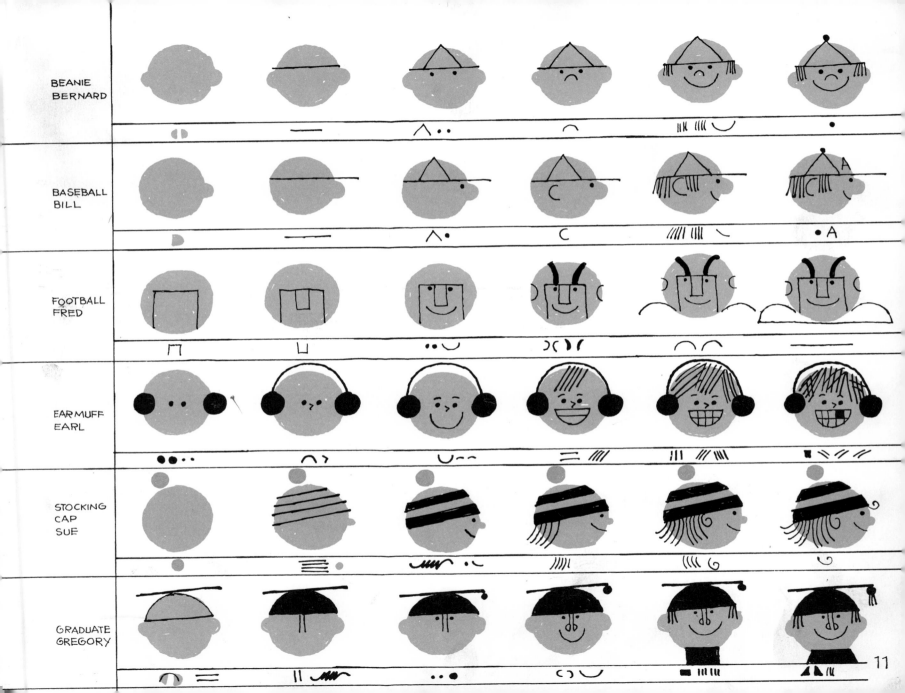

BEANIE
BERNARD

BASEBALL
BILL

FOOTBALL
FRED

EARMUFF
EARL

STOCKING
CAP
SUE

GRADUATE
GREGORY

11

BANDSMAN BEN

ENGINEER ERIC

SCOT SANDY

PIONEER PURVIS

CHEF CHESTER

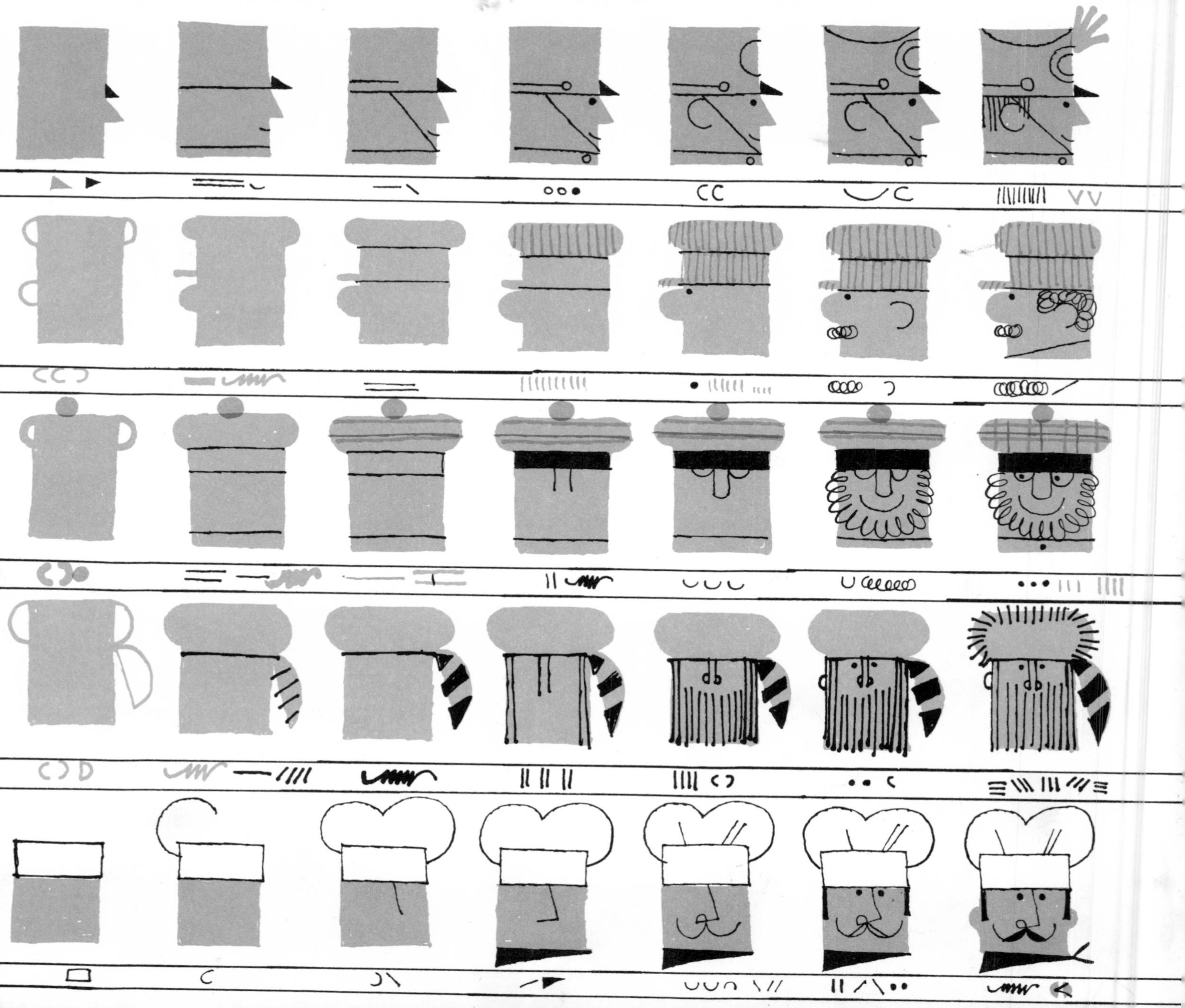

12

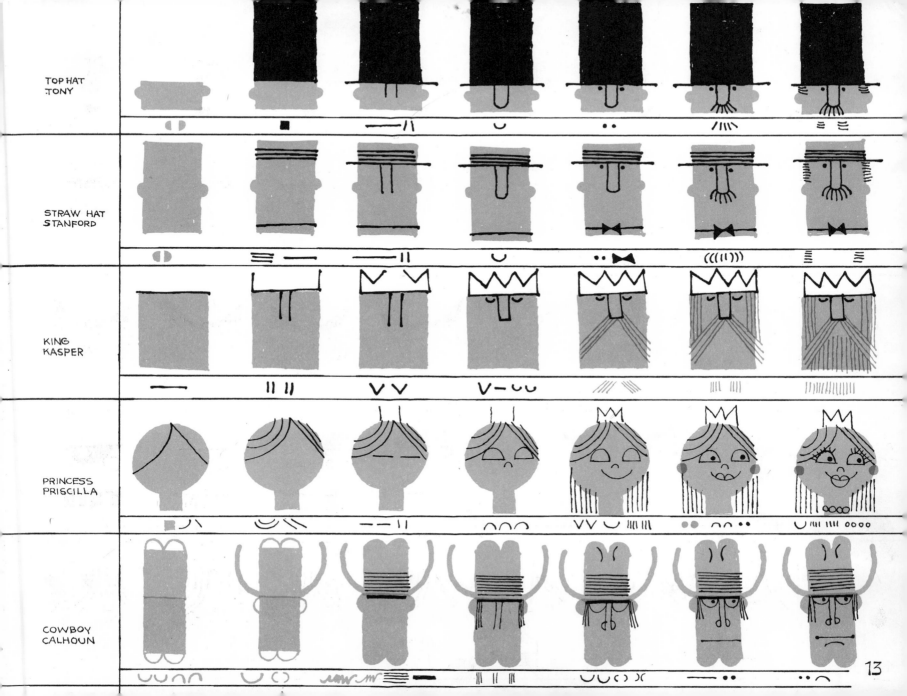

TOP HAT TONY

STRAW HAT STANFORD

KING KASPER

PRINCESS PRISCILLA

COWBOY CALHOUN

13

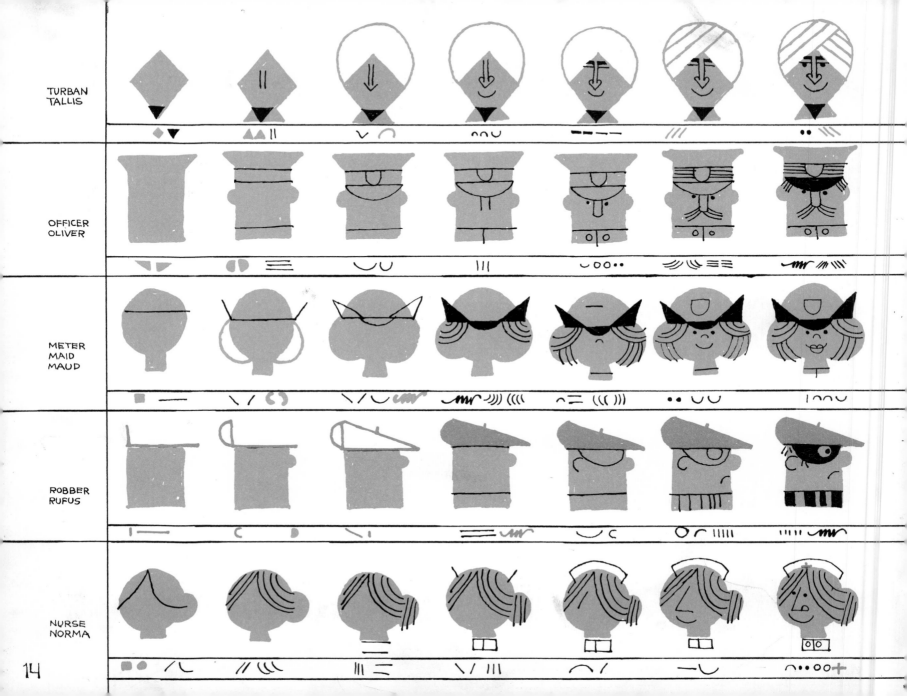

TURBAN
TALLIS

OFFICER
OLIVER

METER
MAID
MAUD

ROBBER
RUFUS

NURSE
NORMA

14

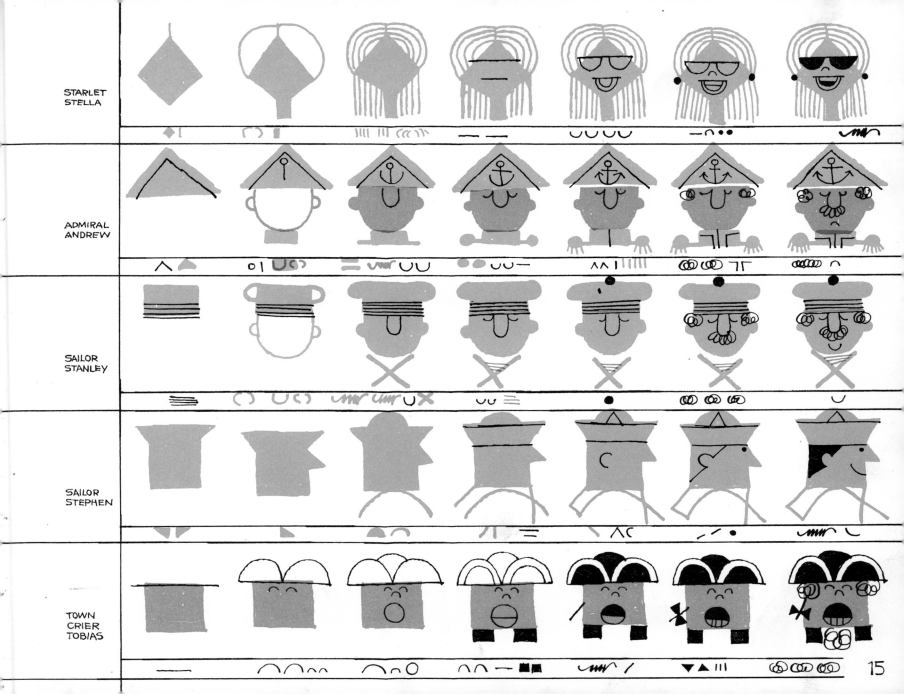

STARLET
STELLA

ADMIRAL
ANDREW

SAILOR
STANLEY

SAILOR
STEPHEN

TOWN
CRIER
TOBIAS

15

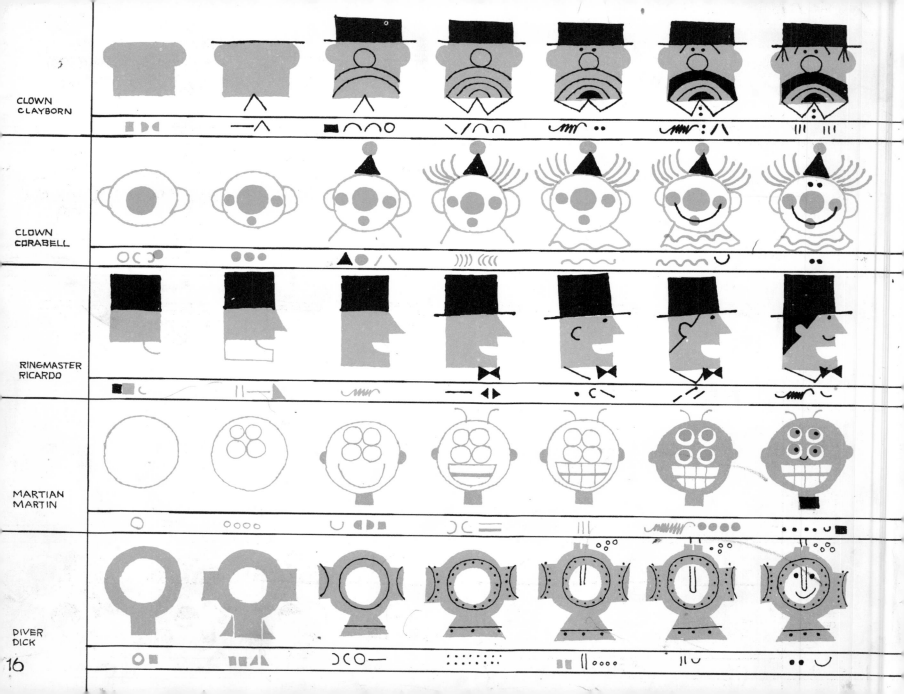

CLOWN
CLAYBORN

CLOWN
CORABELL

RINGMASTER
RICARDO

MARTIAN
MARTIN

DIVER
DICK

16

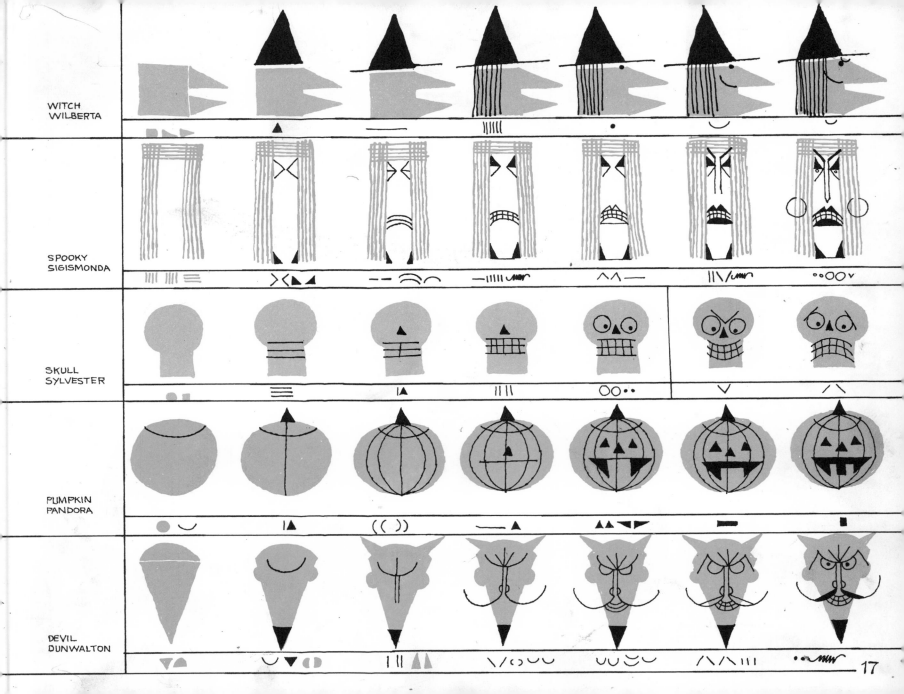

WITCH
WILBERTA

SPOOKY
SIGISMONDA

SKULL
SYLVESTER

PUMPKIN
PANDORA

DEVIL
DUNWALTON

17

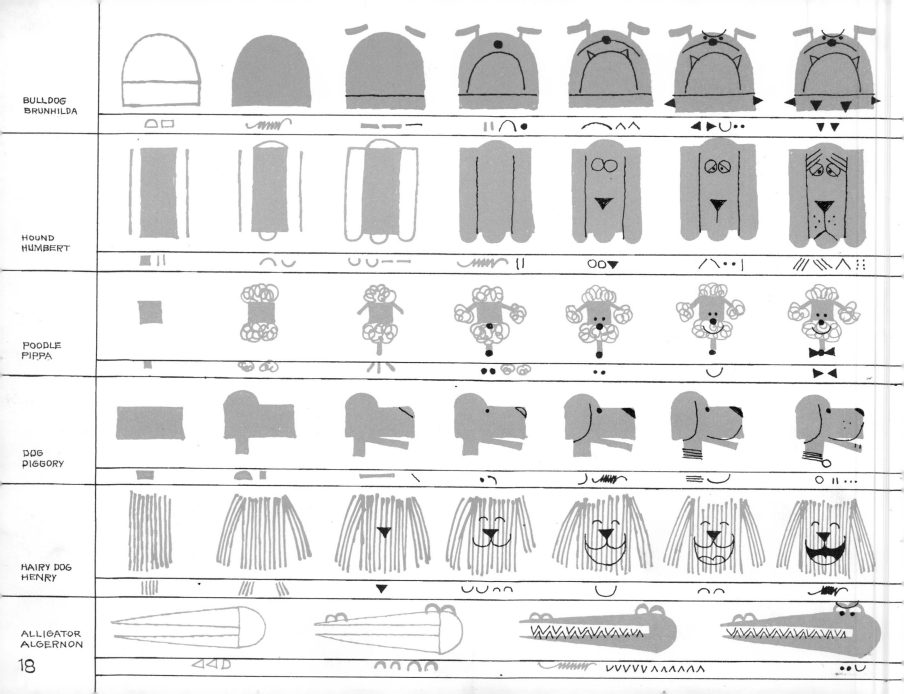

BULLDOG
BRUNHILDA

HOUND
HUMBERT

POODLE
PIPPA

DOG
DIGGORY

HAIRY DOG
HENRY

ALLIGATOR
ALGERNON

18

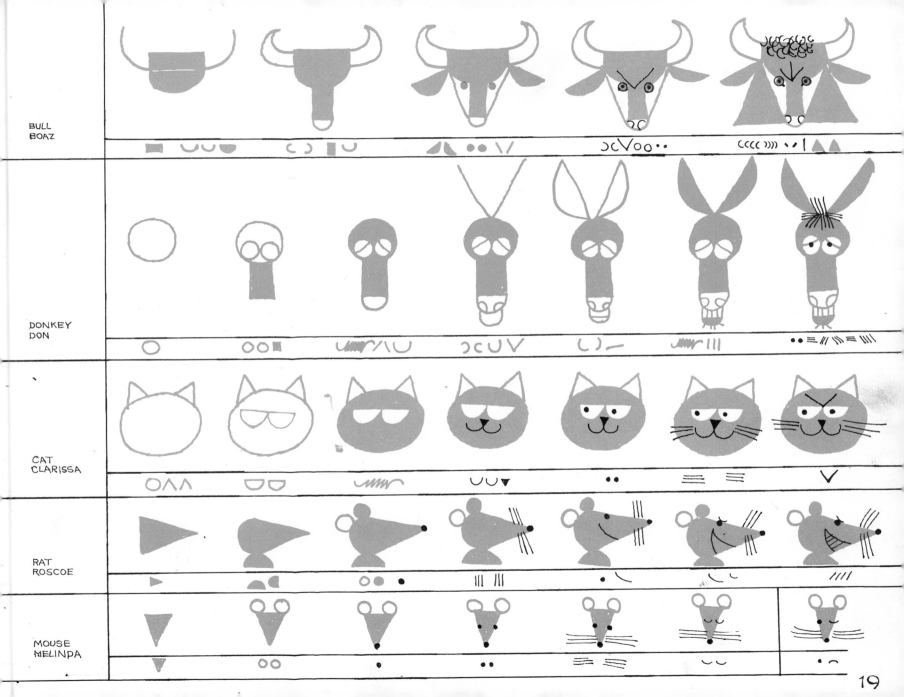

BULL
BOAZ

DONKEY
DON

CAT
CLARISSA

RAT
ROSCOE

MOUSE
MELINDA

19

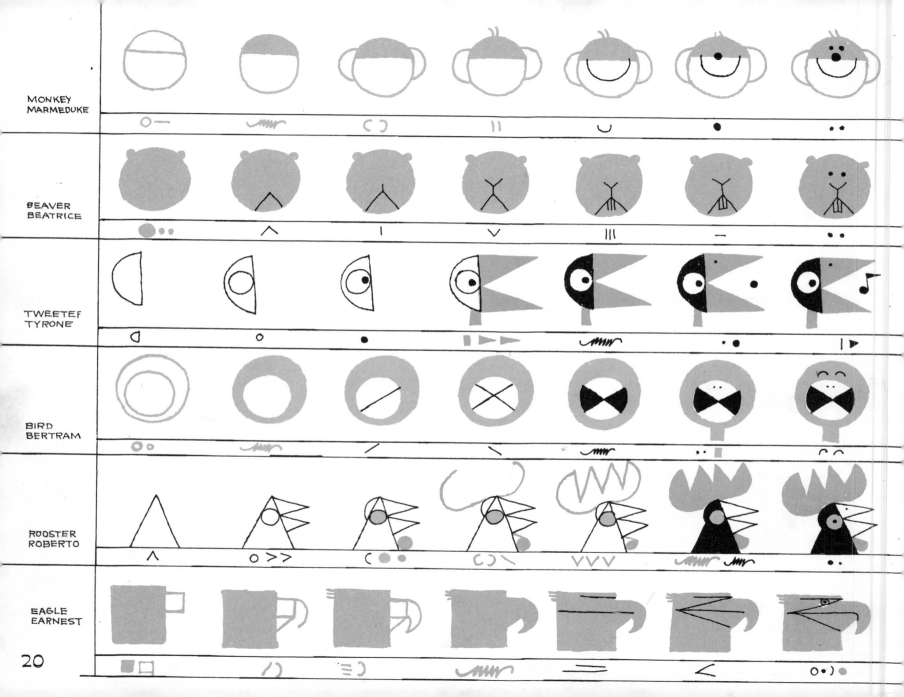

MONKEY
MARMEDUKE

BEAVER
BEATRICE

TWEETEF
TYRONE

BIRD
BERTRAM

ROOSTER
ROBERTO

EAGLE
EARNEST

20

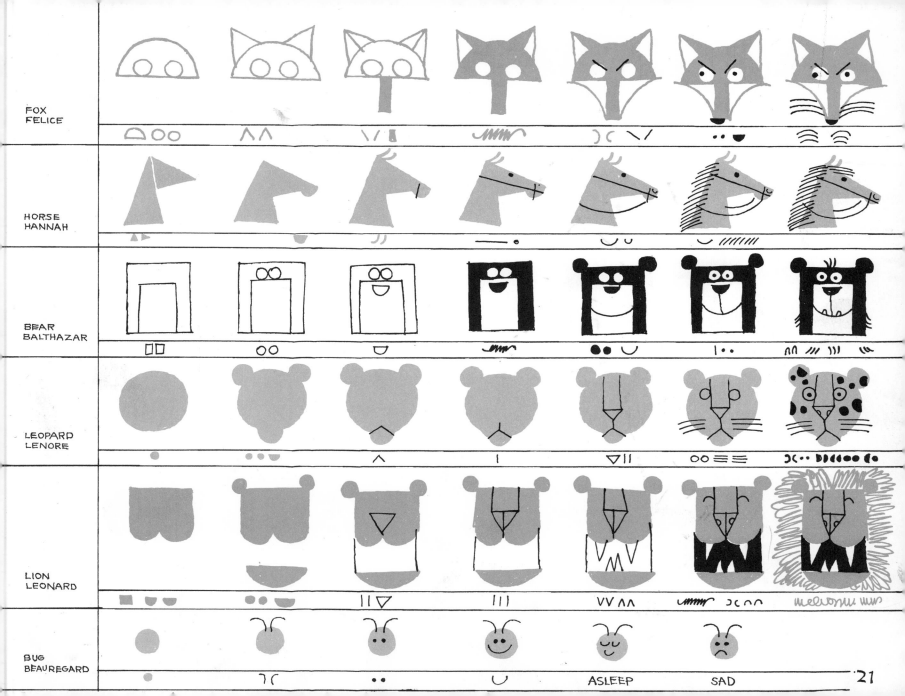

FOX
FELICE

HORSE
HANNAH

BEAR
BALTHAZAR

LEOPARD
LENORE

LION
LEONARD

BUG
BEAUREGARD

ASLEEP   SAD

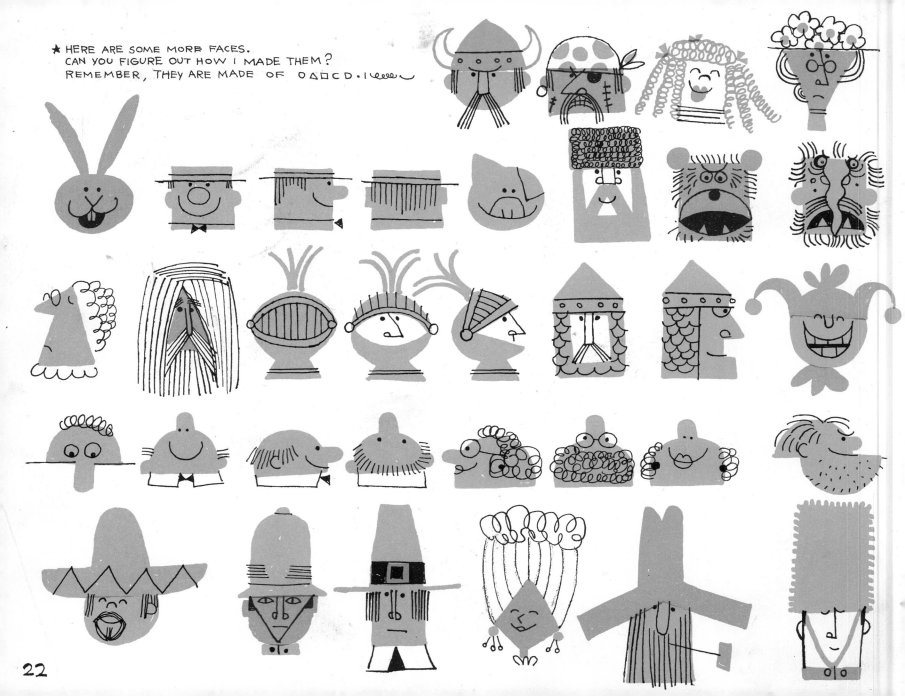

★ HERE ARE SOME MORE FACES.
CAN YOU FIGURE OUT HOW I MADE THEM?
REMEMBER, THEY ARE MADE OF ○△□CD·l〰〰

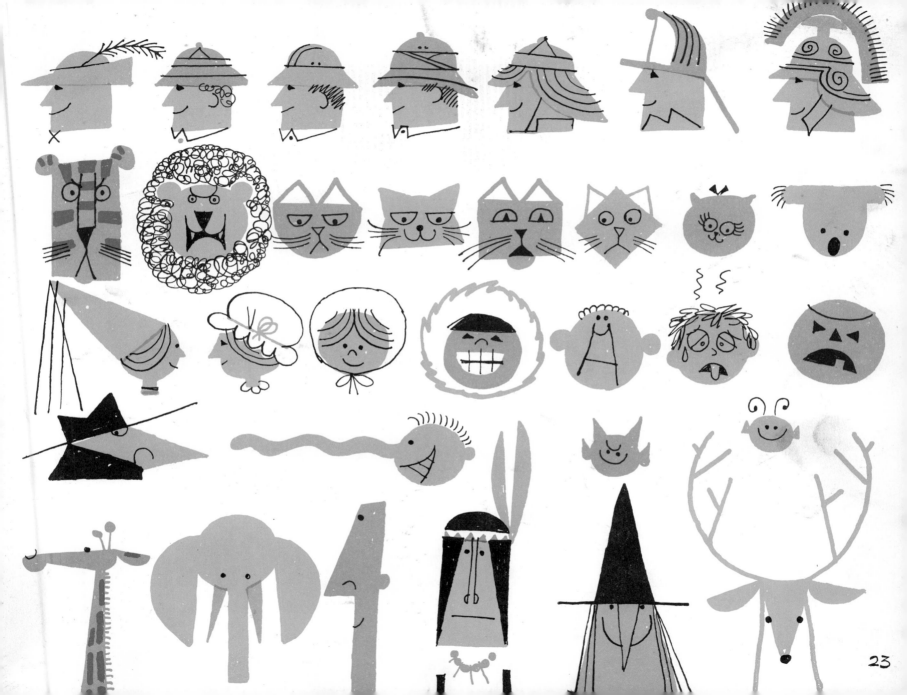

23

- ONE PART OF LEARNING TO DRAW IS TO LOOK AT REAL THINGS, PHOTOGRAPHS OF THINGS AND OTHER ARTISTS WAY OF DRAWING THINGS AND TRY TO DRAW WHAT YOU SEE. ANOTHER PART IS TO TAKE PIECES OF TWO OR MORE THINGS YOU LEARN TO DRAW AND PUT THEM TOGETHER TO MAKE A NEW THING. HERE ARE SOME WAYS FOR YOU TO MAKE "NEW THINGS" WITH THIS BOOK.

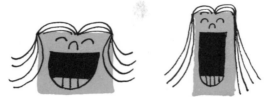

★ YOU CAN MAKE THE SHAPE TALLER...   ...WIDER...OR...

CHANGE IT... FROM SQUARE TO ROUND...

... FROM ROUND TO SQUARE ....OR...

 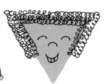 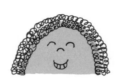 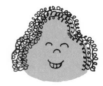

...... DIAMOND,   OR TRIANGULAR,   OR ANY OTHER SHAPE YOU CAN THINK OF.

  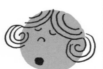 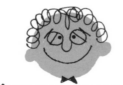 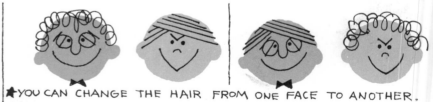

★ YOU CAN CHANGE THE NOSE FROM ONE FACE TO ANOTHER.   ★ YOU CAN CHANGE THE HAIR FROM ONE FACE TO ANOTHER.

   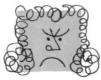   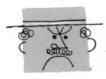

★ MOVING, SWAPPING, ADDING AND SUBTRACTING PARTS ARE ALL WAYS OF MAKING "NEW THINGS".

24

★ MORE NOTES AND HINTS:

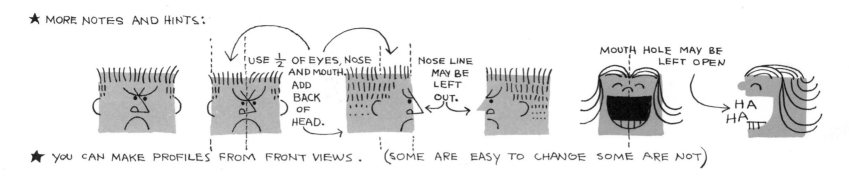

USE ½ OF EYES, NOSE AND MOUTH. ADD BACK OF HEAD.

NOSE LINE MAY BE LEFT OUT.

MOUTH HOLE MAY BE LEFT OPEN

HA HA

★ YOU CAN MAKE PROFILES FROM FRONT VIEWS. (SOME ARE EASY TO CHANGE SOME ARE NOT)

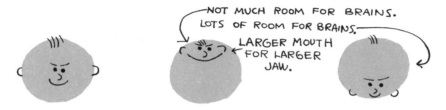

NOT MUCH ROOM FOR BRAINS.

LOTS OF ROOM FOR BRAINS.

LARGER MOUTH FOR LARGER JAW.

★ YOU CAN MOVE THE FEATURES UP TO MAKE THE FACE LOOK TOUGH OR DUMB, OR DOWN TO DO THE OPPOSITE.

* NOTE THAT EARS MOVE DOWN AS EYES AND NOSE MOVE DOWN.

* NOTICE HEAD REMAINS THE SAME SIZE.

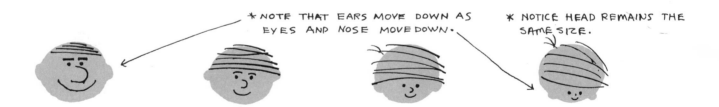

★ TO MAKE A FACE LOOK YOUNGER MAKE THE NOSE AND EYEBROWS SMALLER, ALSO MOVE THE FEATURES DOWN.

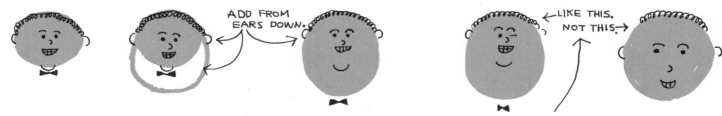

ADD FROM EARS DOWN.

LIKE THIS. NOT THIS

★ TO MAKE A FACE LOOK FAT— KEEP THE FEATURES SMALL, CLOSE TOGETHER AND HIGH ON THE FACE.

25

● HERE ARE SOME PARTS IN CASE YOU WOULD LIKE TO MAKE SOME FACES FROM SCRATCH.

NOSES

EYES

MOUTHS

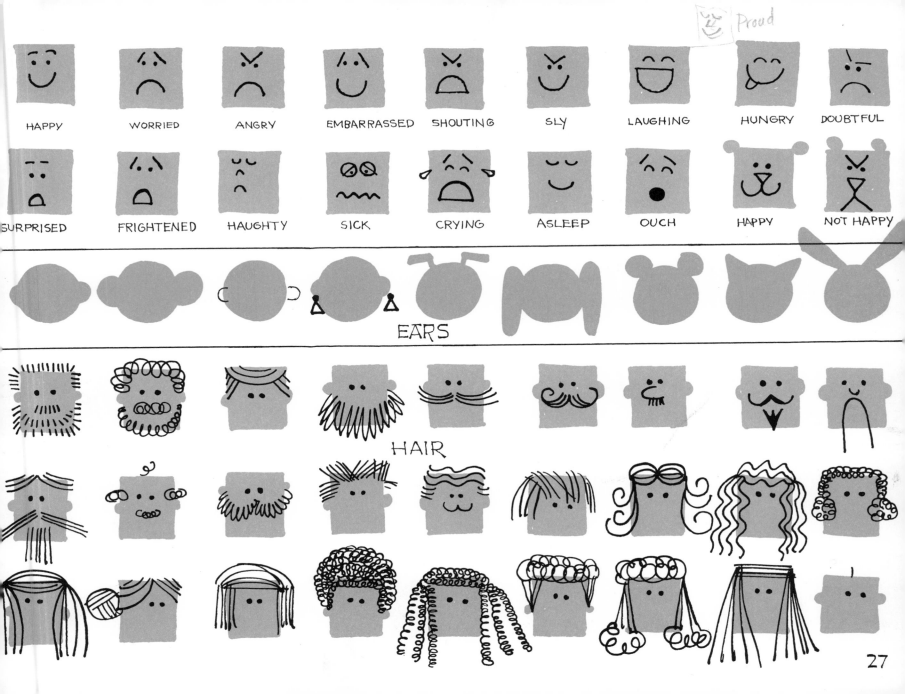

Proud

HAPPY   WORRIED   ANGRY   EMBARRASSED   SHOUTING   SLY   LAUGHING   HUNGRY   DOUBTFUL

SURPRISED   FRIGHTENED   HAUGHTY   SICK   CRYING   ASLEEP   OUCH   HAPPY   NOT HAPPY

EARS

HAIR

27

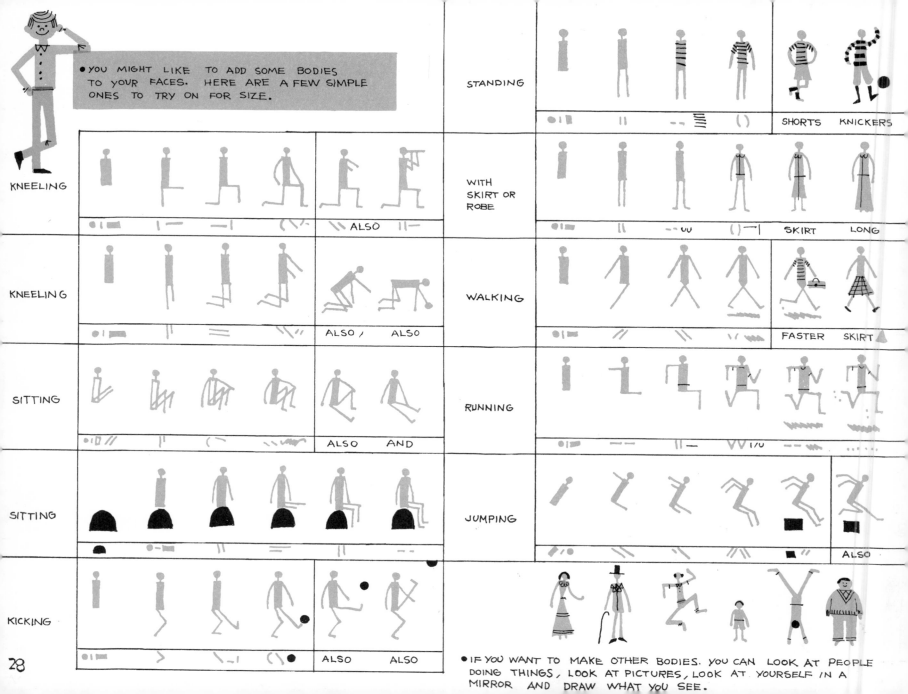

- YOU MIGHT LIKE TO ADD SOME BODIES TO YOUR FACES. HERE ARE A FEW SIMPLE ONES TO TRY ON FOR SIZE.

STANDING

SHORTS   KNICKERS

KNEELING

ALSO

WITH SKIRT OR ROBE

SKIRT   LONG

KNEELING

ALSO   ALSO

WALKING

FASTER   SKIRT

SITTING

ALSO   AND

RUNNING

SITTING

JUMPING

ALSO

KICKING

ALSO   ALSO

- IF YOU WANT TO MAKE OTHER BODIES. YOU CAN LOOK AT PEOPLE DOING THINGS, LOOK AT PICTURES, LOOK AT YOURSELF IN A MIRROR AND DRAW WHAT YOU SEE.

28

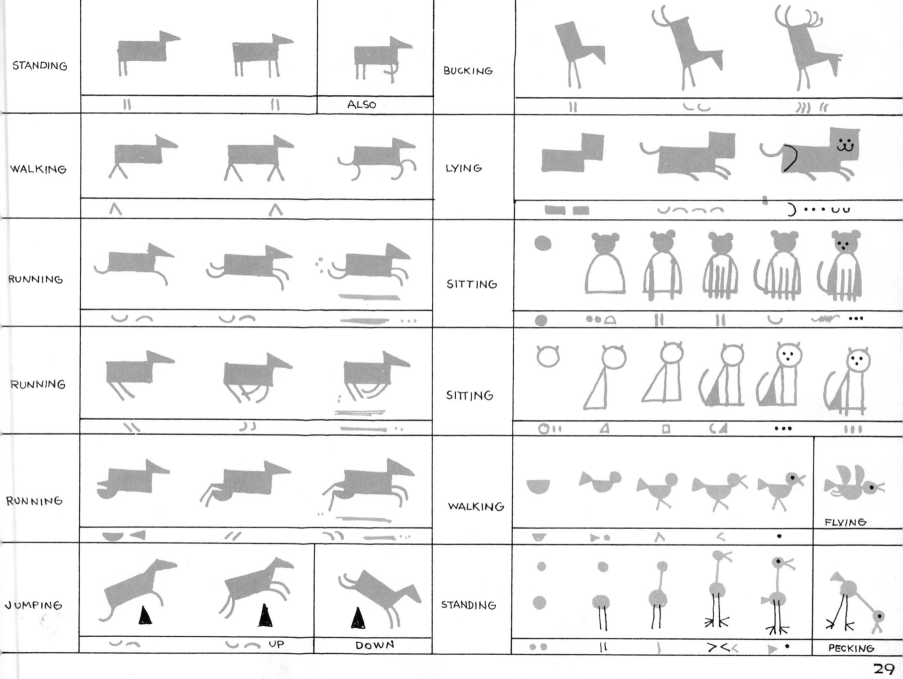

STANDING			BUCKING			
	II	II	ALSO	II	⌣⌣	))) II
WALKING			LYING			
	∧	∧		▭ ▭	⌣ ⌣ ⌣ ⌣	) ... ∪∪
RUNNING			SITTING			
	⌣	⌣		●	●● ⌂	II	II	∪	...
RUNNING			SITTING			
	))	))		O II	△	▢	⊂△	•••	III
RUNNING			WALKING			FLYING
	⌣	//	))	⌣	►●	∧	<	•	
JUMPING		DOWN	STANDING			PECKING
	⌣ UP		••	II	)	><<	►•	

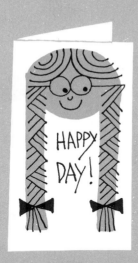

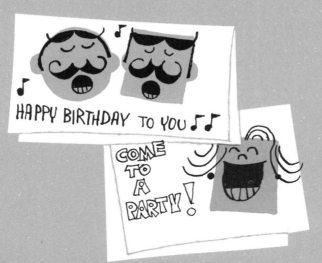

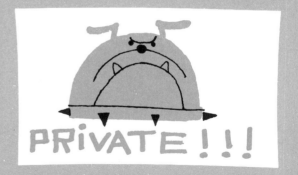

YOU CAN USE FACES TO MAKE ALL KINDS OF GOOD STUFF, SUCH AS:

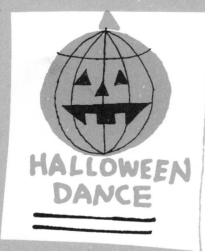

HALLOWEEN DANCE

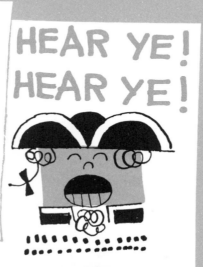

HEAR YE! HEAR YE!

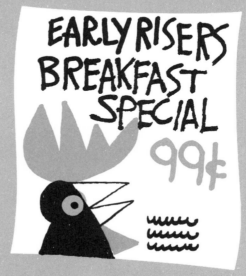

EARLY RISERS BREAKFAST SPECIAL 99¢

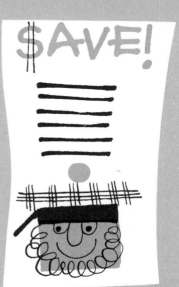

$AVE!

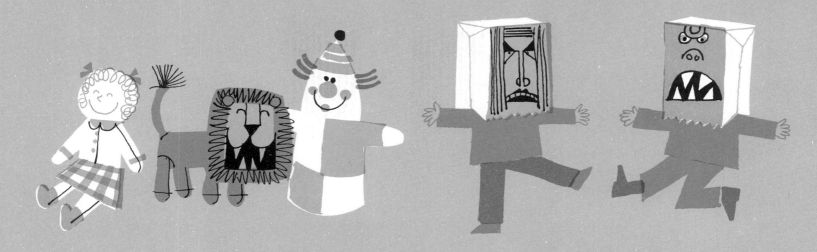

CARDS, SIGNS, POSTERS, LETTERS, MASKS, PUPPETS, AND DOLLS.

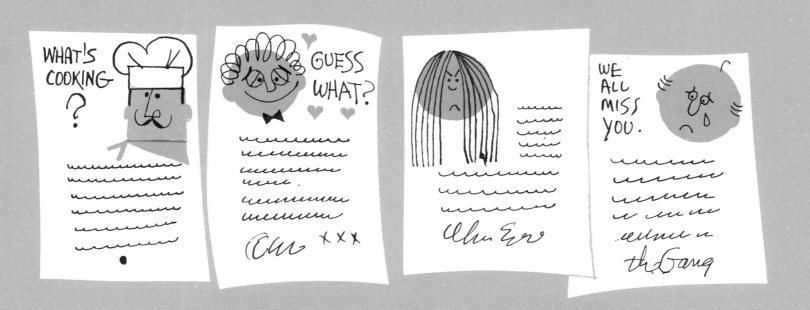

COPYING IS ONE WAY TO LEARN HOW TO DRAW. I HOPE YOU ENJOY
TRYING TO DRAW "MY WAY" CONTINUE TO DRAW "YOUR WAY"
AND KEEP LOOKING FOR NEW WAYS.

HAPPY DRAWING, Ed Emberley

·INDEX·

A
ADMIRAL ANDREW-15
* ALLIGATOR ALGERNON-18
ANGRY ARNOLD-4

B
BABY BONNIE-9
BANDSMAN BEN-12
BARITONE BARNEY-8
BASEBALL BILL-11
BEANIE BERNARD-11
* BEAR BALTHAZAR-21
* BEAVER BEATRICE-20
* BIRD BERTRAM-20
BLACK EYE BOB-9
BRAIDS BARBIE-10
* BUG BEAUREGARD-21
BULL BOAZ-19
* BULLDOG BRUNHILDA-18

C
* CAT CLARISSA-19
CHEF CHESTER-12
CLOWN CLAYBORNE-16
* CLOWN CORABELL-16
CONCEITED CONROY-6
COUNT CLARENCE-8
COWBOY CALHOUN-13
CURLERS CAMILLA-10

D
DETERMINED DAN-6
DEVIL DUNWALTON-17
DIVER DICK-16
DOCTOR DIANE-8
* DOG DIGGORY-18
DONKEY DON-19

E
* EAGLE EARNEST-20
EARMUFF EARL-11
EMBARRASSED EMILY-4
ENGINEER ERIC-12

F
FOOTBALL FRED-11
* FOX FELICE-21
FRECKLES FREDA-9
FRIGHTENED FENWICK-7
FUZZY FRAN-10

G
GIGGLE GERTIE-5
GRADUATE GREGORY-11
GRUMPY GWENDOLYN-6

H
* HAIRY DOG HENRY-18
HAPPY HARRIET-4
HEAVY HARLOW-9
HOLLERING HAROLD-6
* HORSE HANNAH-21
* HOUND HUMBERT-18

K
KING KASPER-13
K.O.'D KARL-10

L
LAUGHING LENA-6
* LEOPARD LENORE-21
LION LEONARD-21
LOVESICK LOU-5

M
* MARTIAN MARTIN-16
MEASLES MICHAEL-10
METER MAID MAUD-14
* MONKEY MARMEDUKE-20
* MONSTER MELVIN-7
* MOUSE MELINDA-19

N
NURSE NORMA-14

O
OFFICER OLIVER-14

P
PIONEER PURVIS-12
* POODLE PIPPA-18
PRINCESS PRISCILLA-13
PROFESSOR PIETRO-9
PROUD PAUL-5
* PUMPKIN PANDORA-17
PUZZLED POLLY-5

R
* RAT ROSCOE-19
RINGMASTER RICARDO-16
ROBBER RUFUS-14
ROOSTER ROBERTO-20

S
SAD SAM-4
SAILOR STANLEY-15
SAILOR STEPHEN-15
SCOT SANDY-12
* SKULL SYLVESTER-17
SLEEPING SIMONE-7
SLY SID-4
SMILING SCOTT-4
SNOOTY SAMANTHA-5
SNORING SALVATORE-7
SPOOKY SIGISMONDA-17
STARLET STELLA-15
STOCKING CAP SUE-11
STRAW HAT STANFORD-13
SURPRISED SYBIL-7

T
TIRED TILLIE-5
TOP HAT TONY-13
TOUGH TOM-9
TOWN CRIER TOBIAS-15
TURBAN TALLIS-14
* TWEETER TYRONE-20

V
VAMPIRE VICTOR-7

W
WHISKERS WALDO-10
WHISTLING WANDA-8
WINKING WILLIE-8
WITCH WILBERTA-17

Y
YODELING YOLANDA-8
YUM YUM YOLAND-6

* FACES STARRED CAN BE
CHANGED FROM MALE TO
FEMALE OR VICE VERSA
BY MERELY CHANGING
THE NAME. FOR INSTANCE,
"MARTIAN MARTIN" COULD
BE CHANGED TO
MARTIAN MARCIA.